The
Incident

The
Incident

E.E. Jones

**STACK
BOOKS**

Smokestack Books
1 Lake Terrace, Grewelthorpe,
Ripon HG4 3BU
e-mail: info@smokestack-books.co.uk
www.smokestack-books.co.uk

ISBN 9781838198831

Smokestack Books
is represented by
Inpress Ltd

*For Mum,
'the still point of the turning
world', beloved Muse and
midwife of these poems.*

Contents

Spring

I walked straight up to winter
being his youngest daughter
and said to him
it's my turn now
the flowers say it is

Direct Action

the flowers have taken this town
and the birds are returning
singing their exiled songs

in many colours
the flowers have risen
not without cost

mourn for the fallen of autumn

remember with sorrow
the snowdrops' fierce stand against frost

but the flowers are holding their ground
and the snow is retreating

the year is ours

The Other God

once
I said I was an atheist
but God laughed in my face

the other God
whose holy writ is a tight wad
in a clenched fist

daily
His tills ring out their hymn
kerching! kerching!

He knows our weight in gold
He weighs us all
against the price of bread

His bailiffs call
the numbers of the overdrawn
all life is debt

now I frequent His altars
furtively
true heretics sit in the gutters

but I stand in line
key in my sin
confess

the ghost in the machine
grants me conditional absolution
as my soul sinks in the red

my balance is found wanting
alas
the damned have no savings

a dropped coin
winks at me from the pavement

truly
His eyes
are everywhere

Sanctioned

when they came for him
I was not there
or anywhere near

though I might have been
in the next street

or an adjacent universe

when he returned
defeated
clutching his crumpled form

what they wanted was
the patch of ground on which he stood

his morning coffee
his shopping list
his right to exist

all this they took
until he had nothing
not even the words

and I was not a friend or neighbour
but only another stranger
who read of his death in the paper
and signed the petition

I did not write to his family
or stand with a placard
protesting in shame
or even
(forgive me)
remember his name

Lord Justice

for my friend, deported 2018

once he was a boy
playing with teddies
and puppets
perhaps

now he sits
in the high
chair

fifteen minutes
is all he needs
to unstring you of hope

and leave you
bereft
collapsed
on the bench

I want to shake him
from his fancy dress

kick away the whole toy box

demand to know
what earthly thing
gives him the right

to reach into your life
and pull you out

For the Shipwrecked

Berlin, 27 February 1933

I felt it listing that night
we set out to protest
but the police turned us back

my father shut himself in his cabin
refused to be moved
wake me when it's over

my wife took my hand

I remember
the clarity of the stars
their remoteness

Europe's glittering flashbulbs
ironic points of light
far away and quite useless

we talked lightly of lifeboats
would not be alarmed
Paris is lovely at this time of year
my uncle's brother has a job in Prague

someone said *taking on water*
somebody cried

I peered over the side at the blackness
imagined its touch
ice or fire
which is worse?

my wife shut her eyes

we clutched each other
on the tilting deck
and wept

Surrender

the end came
and we were still breathing
oh it was strange

the radio crackled
and stuttered to silence
the worst thing had happened

the sun and moon did not disappear
we did not float from the Earth
in a howling vortex of fear

next day was a Friday

so think of us then
swallowing terror and rage
clearing the breakfast things
cycling to work in the rain

a walk in the park
a supper with friends
to mock us with hope
that nothing has changed

not really
not yet
not for us

first we must learn
not to say what we mean
and then not to mean what we say

so think of us now
willing our eyes not to meet
by chance in the street

For the Heroes of Mechelen

in the yard outside
someone's brother is bouncing
a laugh and a ball
on childhood's wall

he's upstairs
kneeling on his mother's floor
filching red tissue paper
from her bedroom drawer

lightheaded with mortality
and with a bravery
he barely understands

he knows he cannot think beyond
the puncture that he'll fix (tonight)
and the lamp he purchased
from the local store
(a German brand)
and he's half boyish still
and wants to laugh

though later he will brush his hand
not quite by accident
over the naked flame

(he wants to know
how much he can stand)

of course
it hurts like hell
the life in him cries out
he wants to live

but now he's lying
on the hard and brittle ground
under the starless void
where heaven might have been

he and two friends
they've placed his red light on the line
but in his heart
he thinks surely
the signal is too small
an obvious fake

until he hears the long scream of the breaks

and he's almost aghast
God and His angels could not stop that train

now he moves
with the speed that comes from the lit fuse
of his own fear

with his father's pliers he hacks
at the wire holding the bolt
on one of the cattle cars
chosen entirely at random

while his friend loses
the few bullets in the single pistol
and then keeps up
a constant volley of rapid shouts
to confuse them
(his friend who one year later will refuse
a blindfold for the firing squad
to die staring death down)

and he knows he would give
the rest of his life
all sixty-five years for the seconds it takes
to slide aside the heavy bolt

as one
two
then a few
dark shapes slip free
quick
quick

the guards are shooting now
and the murderous train is moving

but seventeen stars shine out in the wood

he wants to grab his bike and bolt
Brussels that way
good luck
but a woman
clasps him
holds him

she wants to give him something
everything
for her life
she wants
to thank him

and she who was meat
for the abattoir moments before
is gracious now and queenly

she'll buy him a gift
yes
yes
but what's your address?
she says
how will I find you?

in a dark wood in the middle of a war

incredulous
he finds himself falling awake
in his own bed

yes
he's an old man now
in a new century and this is the gift

this rare and matchless chance
a safe landing

Berlin, 1943

to the memory of Carlo Mierendorff (1897–1943)

the window of the American embassy
glowed gold

outside bone-cold

snow falling like prayers
falling from heaven
and underfoot
hard shards of broken sky

your life weighed less then
than the envelope you carried to a safe address

meanwhile
between the bombs and the Gestapo
cigarettes!

such thin ironic points of light

outside the embassy you paced
and waited for your chance encounter
with a nameless friend

years after your death
his pen
tracing your buried footsteps
in the snow
dug out your laugh
incredulous

your vivid breath signing the air

you thought you knew the rules
you had assumed this place shut up
long since
its windows dark
blank-faced

instead
the silhouettes
of paper-pushers
at their desks

the Swiss somebody said
are taking care of business

what?

inside that neutral square
they walked and talked and worked
a strange facsimile of life
the future or the past?

you stood on the pavement
dropping ash

your nightmare had the thickness
of a sheet of glass

and you a child again
ghosting the pane

Sophie and the History Men

generals and politicians and economists
overshadowed your infancy

they bowed over your cradle
bearing gifts for your twenty-first birthday
promising the Earth

your mother held you close

already outside your window
the hard cold stars
of Fascism
had begun to form

the League of Nations was a bedtime story

each night your father
lit the lamp beside your bed

mother closed the curtains carefully
lest the whispers of war in the constellations
disturb your dreams

already they feared the nightmare
from which they could not protect you

like that knock on the door

The Incident

the fourth of August nineteen forty-four
was the most beautiful day

years later
someone remembered
how the dog on the houseboat barked
and the passers-by with their shopping bags
stopped and stared as if at an accident
then drifted away
shaking their heads

the sky was the same oblivious blue
the dog lapped from a bucket
it had to go on being Friday
and there was plenty to do

women of Amsterdam went on making jam

decades later there would be time enough
to remember and to make a shrine

The Ferryman

had a famous girl in his boat

he wants the world to know
that she was prettier
at fifteen
than in any surviving photo

a model passenger he says
she didn't cry or make a scene
oh no
she came quietly enough

she paid full price

but something that she left on the near bank
robs him of his quiet retirement
and he's aggrieved
he's earned it
after all

how many men
could stand a job like that?

suddenly the world wants answers
and the Austrians have taken
his police bus pass into custody

and it's his stupid fault

he knows
he should have burned the little book

it can't be helped
(he owns a copy now)

Handfast

for Isa Muazu, hunger striker, deported 17 December 2013

think of his starved hand
reaching for England
as they stretchered him towards the exit

his small wrist
helpless
in the terminal darkness

and his thin fingers
through which justice slipped

if you could stand and listen
to his dry lips whispering *freedom*
like a password
his sole prayer
to breathe our English air

then would you hold that hand
England?

I think you would
if it were up to you
though England's grim-eyed guards
say otherwise
and ranks of hobnailed headlines
stand behind them

would you cast off
the newsprint's mailed glove
to save a dying man?

if *you* could choose

I say
you'd take his hand and hold it fast
not letting go

handfast
an English word

A Poem on our Proud History of Welcoming Strangers

In the eleventh [year] of Elizabeth, one Cartwright brought a slave from Russia, and would scourge him cruelly for which he was questioned, and it was resolved that England was too pure an air for slaves to breathe in...
John Lilburne, 1645

now in the sixty-fifth year
of the second Elizabeth
it should be noted

that the title to the air is disputed
and the slave (most likely)
deported

as for the orphaned boy
who touched this shore
aged nine
fleeing the latest war

why he may fill his lungs
with English air
home
school
ten years or so

but when he is nineteen
may be required
to cough it up
sobbing
as they put him on the plane

since freedom to breathe our freedom
is no longer guaranteed

Leave to Remain

for three million (and more)

how for some
this debate
is a pitch
of skill

is a twist
of wit
is a twitch
of thumb

is a play
of words
on screens
in bars

is a game
of nerves
is a house
of cards

but for her
at stake
is the life
of home

and the odds
are long
and the boys
laugh on

as the table
shakes
and her card
is thrown

Salvage

to the memory of Jo Cox (1974–2016)

someone shattered your light
into fragments

fatal

but a crowd came

weeping
they gathered
each spark

they stood in the rain
cupping your light in their hands

as if guarding a promise

Phoenix Park Murders

6 May 1882

another day in the archive of missed chances
where history is folded and at peace

suddenly a paper slips from my grasp
and floats to the floor
the weightlessness of the past!

I bend to retrieve a telegram that speaks
of double murder in the park
pause
to consider how two corpses tipped the scales
towards revenge
the hatred on which History depends

then file it away between recriminations
nation is speaking to nation

there was a boy on a bicycle that day
whose great-grandchildren
still leave flowers on the path
each year
on the sixth of May

in memory of a sunny day gone wrong
a child's shock
his sudden strong dismay
to find two bodies bleeding on the grass

two casualties of a half-forgotten war
whose public deaths mean nothing any more

X

I carry this card

if caught in any unholy equation
remember my 'x'
is the 'x' at the end of a text

not a shard
to bury itself in the heart

or a chip
in some giddy casino of hate

or a number
to feed the exchange rate

I state this now
to avoid all doubt

if they count me in
you must count me out

At the Gates

see the gentle
unbelieving mother
steady her
child's hand

see them waiting
oh so patient
in the long line
of the damned

but who can stand
in the other line
and keep their place
and think it fine

no friend of mine

The Long View

November 1922

silence is golden

one hears things of course
echoes
footfalls
where my people labour
for their latest lords

flash floods
sandstorms
but mostly silence

this is what I like
to drowse in darkness
hiding my dreams from the light

the sun
my father's eye
still scans the valley
preys on every shadowed thing
he can't come in

centuries crumble away
one forgets the names of the gods
the dates of the wars

remembers best
the outline of a well-appointed room
that chest for instance
over there
my chair

these things can wait

to wake at last
in my own time is all I ask

Making an Entrance

Lord C
his daughter Evelyn
the Lady E

in pink
in mauve
in cream
in pale blue

in gloves
in hats
in silks
in all the press

so many entrances!

at summer fetes
at court and at the races

up the aisle in white

something in the mode of entering a room
your mother said
will prove your birth
prove what?

Sir B
and his wife Evelyn
now Lady B

in mourning black

in brown
in green
bright lilac
red velvet
flaming orange

the papers keep your plumage lovingly

in New York
Monte Carlo and Menton

only once
your wardrobe unremarked

only that one night
you crawled into History
through a hole in the wall

and gold... everywhere the glint of gold

Enheduanna

c. 2250 BCE

what I have recited at midnight
they will repeat in the morning
four thousand years from now

this is my space

tell them
my father was king
but my mother came of the conquered race

tell them
of innumerable generations stilled
how our cities fell to silence like a plague
the minds of the great dissolved
like smoke in the wind

tell them
I danced for the Goddess
the day we stopped time
plucked a bird from the air
and made it a sign

how the words flowed on our lips
like water
like wine

tell them
there are stones singing in the desert
four thousand years from now
though the rivers have altered their ways
and the hills are changed

and many will stand
in an unknown land
under different stars

and know my name

Unpublished

reader
I have pitched our tent
here
under mounds of fresh fallen
paper

nothing to do
but wait a few years
for someone
to dig us out

indifference is a blizzard

reader
(between the lines)
I begin to fear
you are no more than a mirage
(no offence)

I set out
with the courage
of a fresh sharpened pencil

now I'm down
to my last metaphor
half a biscuit

reader
I ought to post
this poem

dear reader
I know there are other magazines...

it is not heroic to sit here
tasting the luminous defeat

but I do not think I can help it

Interview

scorned by the panel
more rapport with the pot plant
dead in the corner

Symptoms

lately
doctor
it's been happening again

leaving the office headfirst
not full-blown vanishing fits
but visibility issues

fellow sufferers will know
how disconcerting it is
to sit at your desk
quietly evaporating
or worse be in a meeting
and feel your edges blurring

colleagues have mentioned
occasional fuzziness
and sometimes I have to leave early
before they see right through me

also I'm afraid of leaving wisps of myself
on buses (quite embarrassing)

I haven't yet disclosed
transparency at work
fearful that they'll never
catch my drift

now I'm wondering
can you give me a sick note
or better
a prescription?

Cheetah

see that
streak of fire
in the grass

that's mother
looping her prey
in a Gordian Knot

but Chinzvi
(her daughter)
is gentle

licking
the world in the face

does not seem to know
just yet
what Nature demands

not quite the image
of her spotted god (maybe)
though she has teeth and claws
as good as any

her sisters pile in for the kill
but she hangs back
one paw on the antelope's flank
looking puzzled

Eden might have suited her better

Climate Summit

item – resolved:
to keep on doing as we did before
the tab's still open

charge it to the poor

The Moderate

it is not easy
this causeway I walk
with my eyes half open
my head half bowed

what if I see something that can't be unseen?

I know by the dull thud in my blood
that this life is conditional

and I am one of the lucky ones
to whom sufferance has been granted
so I accept the terms of the licence

I pledge myself
to the illusion of freedom
though it is not much
it is enough

I have modest hope of a modest income
for this I must do what the world demands

what *can* I do
but despise these others
these heretics
who walk with their eyes wide open?

they would bring me to shame
to grief

what I fear is the voice
that calls me from sleep

the words that compel me to speak

In Retrospect

of course
we'd have been for Alfred
and unity (not Mercian supremacy
or Little Wessex)

back then we'd have added
more clauses to Magna Carta
seen the point of the Peasants' Revolt

we'd have stood with the Levellers in Burford
linked arms with the martyrs at Peterloo
Amritsar
Sharpeville
and Derry

we'd have been the only Chartists
in the village
the first to call out old Lord Macaulay
who (with Cambridge
Westminster
and the Privy Council
all behind him) decried universal suffrage
as 'incompatible with civilisation'

we'd never have swooned into war
pro patria mori
or sat in the stalls at Olympia
praising the autobahn as we waited for Mosley
or poured over the blacklist
murmuring darkly

just picture us then
abolitionists
reformers
repealers
home rulers
suffragettes all...

naturally
times have changed

these days
you'll find us holding the middle ground

the status quo
now
is basically sound

Peterloo Survivors, 1884

but from this distance
you might almost be
veterans of Naseby
or Thermopylae...

a ring of uprights
with a furrowed dignity
at once antique and homely
like Stonehenge

this photograph's
the colour of tea
and so we like our past
sugared and milky
not too hot

the worst evades our gaze

if we could see into your dreams
we'd have a glimpse of something
out of reach

the cost of Liberty
the price of Speech

Anne Sans Tête

Shall I die without justice?

yes but...

there are flowers on the scaffold now
while grass grows in the tiltyard
and it's funny how that happens
isn't it?

we're reading all the heretics
the sycophants are out of print
(the saints are all unreadable
these days)

and there's laughter in the classroom
at your husband's fabled carcass

yes
it's funny how that happens
in the end

Tyndale

in his penultimate darkness

sat with the book
of night on his lap

caressing its
cold spine

(the hours
tightly bound)

how he pleaded
in pliant Latin

for a lamp
let there be lyghte

Rosa's Mockingbird

'And, since it had to happen, I'm happy it happened to a
person like Mrs. Parks.'
Martin Luther King, Jr.

the Goddess of History
has strange favourites and so
the middle-aged woman who sits on the bus
is looking at the bird on her shoulder
that only she can see

strange
how it swooped
through the window

stranger still
she thinks it absurd
how none of the other passengers
say a word

but she is used to being ignored

already its gentle weight
makes her sit taller
as it fixes her now
with its wise amber eyes

she studies the radiance of its wings
she's wondering if it sings

for she knows
it would sound like no other bird
ever heard

as the stranger approaches
she's thinking
how strange
should it choose to open its beak

the moment he tells her to give up her seat

Athene and Odysseus

she might have picked him
from his unripe life
and hung him in the sky
holding him there
with tiny silver shards
so that his shape
shone out among the stars
(ignoring his wife and child
their minute cries)

she might have shredded him
with a single glance
for looking at her sideways
a goddess
impossible-eyed

she might have netted him
from the sea
(as easily
as did that silly
laughing nymph Calypso)
ignored his gasping protest
held him down
force-fed him bliss
while he was choking grief
whispered immortal longings
in his ear

she might have exiled him from himself
as a bird or a beast or a fish
for her amusement

she might have rolled
his luck in a cup on High Olympus
lost his bones in a bet
sighed
then paid the forfeit of his little life
and blown his candle out

she might have plucked
preserved and pickled him

she might have done all this
and if she did
the Universe itself would not object

she was God's daughter
to her fingertips
and these same fingers held his thunderbolt

she might
she might

instead

she swatted arrows from his side as a mother brushes
flies from her sleeping child

smoothed sweet evening's cool into his skin
when he was sleepless

held her hand over his head
to blunt the spear-sharp sun

wrung the sky's limp cloth to catch a drop
to wet his burning lips

watched his feet
printing the dust
underwrote each step

and when he fell
just once
beneath Troy's wall
(his fist closing on emptiness)

threw back the day's bright orb like a lost ball
to his quick hand
and saw him stand
reborn

promised no dangerous reward
fool's gold
or devil's bargain
offered not a day beyond
his natural span

but held the horses of the dawn for three nights
while he lay becalmed at last
in his wife's arms

and turned her grey immortal eyes away

Little Owl

Athene noctua

the day he died
she shrank into herself
one bright unbearable morning

fell
into herself
and kept on falling

Penelope and Telemachus sat up late
keeping his memory warm
death anchored them
to his bed
his bow
his chest
his empty chair

so they mourned
but Life stayed with them
patient as a dog
licking their hands
and nudging for attention

this was their portion being mortal

hers was eternity
she did not want or need
her days unspooling like an endless skein

Athene
leaving the mountain
turning her back on the sun...

nightly now
her wraith-cry
startles the stars

Solar Gravity

for KJJ

yours is the love
I long to fall towards
on lonely star-strewn nights
when far away

and like a distant planet
cold
remote
I turn my face towards the sun
and hope

yours is the love that holds me in my course
when I am weightless
floating in despair
apparently adrift in boundless dark
and hostile comets loiter in my path

yours is the love that saves my flailing heart
within the steady arc of your embrace

you are the one that loves me
through and through
the imperfections of each changing phase

and at my core is simple awe of you
love's magnitude
the force that keeps me true

Motherland

thank you for the four rivers of Eden
for showing them to me

we lived there once
under the whisper of a benign star
the love that points to truth

thank you
for the safe contours of your heart's country
in which we grew

citizens
of a good and gracious land

we lived there once
before I met the world

Fairy Tale

born to be rich
she started early

found the end of the rainbow
tripped
and met a witch

sold her sister
for the pot of gold

and sauntered home
for tea

Kaleidoscope

'This is a moment to seize. The kaleidoscope has been shaken.
The pieces are in flux. Soon they will settle again. Before they
do let us re-order this world around us.'
Tony Blair, 2 October 2001

is this the argument from design?
not Paley's watch this time
but Blair's kaleidoscope

for surely God
is in there somewhere
with the wheat and chaff
and flakes of dust?

observe the ashes rise and re-emerge
as feathers of the warbird
watch and learn

such fearful symmetry!
turn it again
more cities rearranged
the little pieces dancing on command

study the pattern
watch the shifting sand
Bin Laden to Baghdad's
a sleight of hand

collude with history
give it a shake
go on
your fingers itch

Freedom of Speech

not democratic he said
no
not always
not necessarily
not especially democratic
but effective government is what we need

and the lights never dipped
reader

his wife never blinked

not a fly stirred in the hall
the air was scented and cool
the canapés snug on their trays

he smiled
whiter than white
and the audience purred

not a spot on his tie
reader

not a crease in his shirt
sleek
sleek

then I thought
of the place where they iron dissent
from the State

I thought
of the sweaty palms in the night
and the fetid air in the cell
where his words are a brick in the teeth

not democratic
no
no
but effective

then the blood-gag in her mouth
and the crisp cheque in his fist

Realpolitik

after Chilcot

mostly we are patient
we wait in line
we arrive on time
we offer up our lives
our sleepless nights

daily
hourly
we sacrifice to the international oligarchy
and in return we may live

our patience is food on the table
is perilous safety

and when they say
you are the virtuous
the hardworking
for your sake we punish the undeserving
we see them smirking

but this is their world
so we pay the price they name

and when they say
we will keep you safe
by exporting the terror
we are silent
mostly
though we know some will die

they say we are so proud of our boys

we don't want the pavement
to disappear in a sheet of flame
we don't complain

meanwhile their balance increases

but this is not enough
the daily service of our hands and feet
our lip service even

oh no
we must bless the arrangement

they ask us to accept our debt
and be grateful
they own everything anyway
what more can we give them?

we must acknowledge their good faith

Brüning at Harvard

his world shrank to a classroom
History a parade
under the technicolor blue
American post-war skies

odd to think of him
amid the suntanned colonnades
wrapped in his shadows

an ocean between him
and the dead cities
the mass graves

still unforgiven
unforgiving

how he flinched from everything
even the touch of spring
the birds' untranslatable babble

Herr Professor
liked students best at a distance

later they remembered
the quiet violence of his marking
his parched heart's scorched earth economics
and his certainty that he was right

also
the way he walked
head bent
to ward off the whispers

yes him
the Hunger Chancellor
the predecessor

Sisyphus

had known these devils
long before they were made gods
and he their prisoner

back then
he felt the times tremble
and knew what it meant
that Truth alone has no weight
Justice is easily swayed

when the scales are shaken
the balance must fall to the powerful
always

and so they watched him
loading the scale against them
day after day
with all that he had

night after night
he packed his whole life
into crates on the scale against them
right down to the weight of the medal on his chest

then stepped onto the scale himself

and felt the shock of his life
as the whole lot went up
and he was suddenly weightless
worthless
trapped in the heap
of their spoils

now in the camp
they make him bend in the dirt
between beatings
to collect small stones in a bucket
that is emptied daily

this labour amuses the guards
they enjoy wasting him

he knows each stone is a favour returned
for a well-aimed word
a taunt or a gibe
a bright sharpened truth
that he'd flung against them
while there was still time

to the memory of Kurt Schumacher (1895–1952)

1914

here I sit
in History's easy chair

watching you Sylvia
on your hands and knees
in Parliament Square

(where today
your statue does not stand)

literally crawling
slow as Democracy

(they'd stretchered you this far
to lead the deputation)

weak from prison and tube feeding

and to greet you
Keir
who stoops to take your hand
and whispers something
we cannot hear

his mind is full
of the coming war

the curse of flags and hunger

Big Ben is sounding
the old lie
normality

nothing about this is normal

think of Asquith
prime minister

(whose steel gag you wore)

how this moment
he is drafting a missive to the foreign secretary

his writing neat as barbed wire

Behind Enemy Lines

from an anecdote by Carl Zuckmayer

some of us at war
found vent
in poetry

not me

I was afraid
that to fix words
to certain things I'd seen
would make them permanent

trusting the silence more

and afterwards
when any praised
the power of verse
it seemed absurd
or worse
a fraud

no poem
ever shook me like shellfire

but one thing I will tell you
how a friend of mine
guarding some British prisoners

found one of them
an Indian by look of him
so badly wounded
poor man
marooned outside his language

his eyes were moving
but they had no means to tell him
that what the doctors were attempting
wasn't meant to hurt him

God knows
what he'd been told
about the enemy

but anyway

my friend
being desperate
and having nothing
no morphine
even

pulled from the air
the name of the Nobel Laureate
and poet
Rabindranath Tagore

repeated like a chant

Tagore
Tagore
Tagore

oh the look
of sudden wild relief
on that man's face
among the bloody cloths

I wasn't there
but when I heard of that
then something broke

I might have given up on words
almost
but for that moment

The Quality of Mercy

to the memories of WH Auden and Erika Mann,
married 15 June 1935

Malvern Link and Great Malvern
two stations both alike in dignity

alike enough
to confuse the hurried refugee
already bemused by England's
downcast eyes and missing teeth
but gallantly resolved
to be enchanted
escaping the glamorous hell
of capsizing late-Weimar Berlin
and the Nazi-shadowed lands

she came to be married
to an Englishman
sight unseen
a gay poet who offered his name
for her visa
as one might offer a seat on a train

but she
stepping out
at the wrong Malvern station
cabaret star
short-haired and trousered
clutching a sepia postcard
greeted the one man waiting
with impetuous gratitude
(in a thick German accent)
so good of you to marry me!

all this methinks is pure Shakespeare
a problem play
or a late play
the usual mistaken identity
gender confusion
sudden snatched redemption
ending in marriage

and the bride of course
with the eyes of a heroine
and the courage
nightly sticking her pin
in the hide of the *schweinhund*
nightly dancing on the pinhead's
bright ironic point of light

(when they raided the building
she met them on stage
dressed in their uniform
played them for laughs
while the audience fled)

as for the bridegroom-hero
he too knew what it was
to be illegal
understood the looming tragedy
beneath the furtive comedy
of a life lived partly in corners

cultivated a careful eccentricity
useful insouciance

(at the posh school
poetry became his alibi
for nights spent in the garden shed
with the gardener)

poetry makes nothing happen
so he said
but when the obscene Reich bellowed
and he saw the space beside him
in the lifeboat-island
where a wife might sit
was it not poetic to do as he did?
what are buggers for?

everyone in this story is slightly heroic
that's why I like it
even the man on the platform
(whoever he was)
backing away so politely
from the strange foreign lady
and her seeming proposal
not forgetting to thank her

and later the bored registrar
whose sublime indifference
to the groom's suspicious ignorance
of the bride's full name age and place of birth
made everything easy
he would have married me to the poker

did not this betoken a noble resistance
to the claims of Authority?
(or maybe of course he was lazy
no matter!)

poetry makes nothing happen
perhaps
but how strange that
Goebbels in his sound and fury
should choose the very day
of the makeshift ceremony
in sleepy Ledbury in rainy England
to tear out her name from the book of the saved

not knowing by what sleight of hands
of rings
his prey had escaped

the loophole big on her finger

his vengeance undone (for once)
displaced
by the quiet laughter of three almost-friends

the poet
his wife
and his lover the gardener
drinking champagne in the rain

Civil Defence

from the memoir of Fireman Stephen Spender

so there I was cleaning toilets
for England
least I could do

and the lads
decent
not a bad crew
nothing like school (shudder)
or Oxford

the working classes don't seem to mind so much
if one is a bit odd
probably dropped on the head
done time
or down on the luck

they would call one 'sir' not 'comrade'
which was a shame
and as for the wireless
(I'd have flushed the thing if I could)
nothing to do all day
but listen to the Light Programme
and wait for the sky to fall
(sometimes you wished it would)
it was that or ping pong
(I became quite good)

we'd done the different types of bomb
early on
but it was the lecture on gases that did for me
the veils of hell
described so clearly
I can still smell...

this one is like hay he said
and that *like pear drops*
over-sweet
another was *carnations*
I remember

all fatal

and who turns these scents against us?
like being asphyxiated by a rainbow
or murderous birdsong
makes you think
no?

afterwards I stood in a phone box
(that small facsimile shelter)
not for long
just a few moments
until I stopped shaking

I did not lift the receiver
but stood as though listening for something
(the future maybe?)

anyway I went back
and they were quite cheerful
the kettle whistling all clear

got a light sir? want a cuppa?
and the wireless tinkling jazz
like warm summer rain
I swore then not to complain
about that bloody noise
ever again

National Hero

but I'd prefer a statue
of the child you were

how your eyes flared incandescent
in the classroom

when your teacher
mocked the boy absent because
it was his brother's turn to wear the shoes

how you hurled the lesson back
and would not stand to be caned
but went on fighting like a
tiny Glyndŵr

wrong class
wrong voice
wrong age

but the rightness of your rage
confounded them

into shocked silence

to the memory of Nye Bevan (1897–1960)

Another England

beyond the castellated shires
and city towers
the people dream as they always did

freedom is lost and found
equivocal

exiles hiding from their lives
find common ground
on Saturdays
dig deep
share sandwiches in tinfoil
swap seeds

a sudden storm
waters the grassroots
and illuminates the marginal
as summer's embers cool

the sun-filled apples swell
and green turns gold

such heady scent of hope
ripens the heart
and now the time-turned fruits
begin to fall

Doorstepping

the moon beckons

I follow
with my canvass bag
seeding each letterbox

(good evening)

noting the totems
of an upturned bike
a child's tiny slide

(may I ask...)

hope is dragging my heart

the crisscross
swash and backwash
tidal

(are you registered?)

such an art
tonight
to imagine the possible

(can we count on your support?)

hard enough to conceive
a rope of invisible moon-pull
making the ocean heave

(thank you)

to believe

Hope

another throwaway day

life's median hum
no sirens

on the top deck
treetops flickering

two loudmouth lads at the back
conjure your name from the air
bounce it between them

he's all right yeah

an old man
crumpled over his crossword
looks up

smiles
at the woman in the opposite aisle
holding a child

and the girl in the seat behind
with the notebook and the elsewhere eyes
slides her gaze sideways

sees a feather fall from the future

light as a breath

7 June 2017

Polling Station

one year
in every few
we weigh ourselves
and are found wanting

queue
in common space
eyeing our neighbours warily

skirting the noticeboards
imploring help with last month's fete

(we'd come here
if there was a flood
to sit on plastic chairs
sipping small kindness
out of paper cups)

fragile prefabricated State
keeping the wind off
just
but not enough

we cross ourselves and wait

On the Journey Down

football
illnesses
the weather
Tories out
and a whip-round for the driver
is your branch paying for this coach?
what happened to that banner?
our treasurer's a decent old stick
but you can't get the money
housing lobby on Friday
no that was last week
read this it's appalling
listen up! can I speak?
everyone?
put your mobile down
if you're not on this list
(legible please)
pass it round
and say if you're not coming back
'cos we don't want to wait
(sorry again I was late)
show of hands for the radio
can I borrow your pen?
I think I signed this already
absent friends
she moved he went a bit odd
like what?
stopped coming to meetings
what was his name?
I forgot
remember that year the EDL came?
all fifteen of them
bastards
Cable Street it was not
were you there?

Jeremy in our car that time
you remember
I knew him back in the day
of the Haringey Planning Committee
not many of us then on the Left
but he listened to me
were you at that meeting?
actually I was the Chair
canvassing stories
letterboxes
dogs
Lib Dem in Thame was bitten by a cat
years back
he could be in by Christmas
(but we reckon she'll hang on
all the same)
sorry what was your name?
want a mint?
anyone need to stop?
love you don't think *we* have that banner in our loft?

speech choked off
eyes fixed
silence drifting from the blackened tower
acrid silence

1 July 2017

Aftermath

to the memory of Khadija Saye (1992–2017)

still it continues

laying waste to every day

taking the breath
of all you might have said

and blackening
your future canvasses

no-one saw the moment
it reached your grandchildren
asleep
(some forty years from now)

and snuffed them out

Geography

to the memory of Maria Brontë, died 6 May 1825, aged 11

like a fabled land

the vast horizon
of your unmapped talent

forever out of sight
to the sisters who followed

and scaled the heights

driven always by the thought
of silence unredeemed

blank sheets laid out
in preparation for eternity

while you lay still
as a pencil in a box

For an Unknown Migrant

above the spinning globe
the astronaut
clings to a narrow rail

he's holding on
with everything he has
to all he's ever known

as angels stand on pinheads
so he stands
and turns
and treads on emptiness

our breath upholds each step

if he should fall
and lose his footing in the Universe
I think the shock of it would shake the poles

from here the lands are vague and borderless

look down
o voyager
and further down

they're burying a man without his name

a fellow traveller whose grip was good
who trod the waves
while he had strength to tread

then slipped
and felt his fist closing on emptiness
and broke his mother's heart

no greater grief was there in all the world

For the Stansted 15

words can only take
so much weight

a man
falls
through
the poem

arms outstretched

no line of mine
can hold him

but you took
the weight of the times

with your whole lives

Could Do Better

not the most encouraging start
I note
but they are learning
knowledge spreads like fire

this term has seen
some creative progression
an attempt to fix their shadows
through painting

words came lately
now they are naming
everything
even the stars

hatred translates
too easily
love is the harder language
between tribes

although social
their taste for building walls
may prove incurable

also I have observed
a fatal tendency
to believe in almost anything
except themselves

playtime is difficult
alarming

(their songs I must say
are charming)

moments ago
they were only counting
now they are splitting atoms

if they could subtract
the instinct to divide
they might survive
(otherwise doomed)

by the way
did I mention they have been to their moon?

Still Life

for a critically endangered stick insect

feather-light

the weight
of an unblemished
soul

so slight a life
you'd think Atlas would
never know the difference

but her death
would hang most
heavy

being the lone
parenthesis
between her kind
and extinction

curled in your hand

she has folded
six legs with the dignity
of the vanquished

and if her eggs
should fail

the meek
inherit nothing